Table of contents

ANIMAL CHILDHOOD

Have you ever wondered what the childhood of animals looks like? How their parents take care of them so that they're safe from enemies but at the same time can learn everything necessary? Well, it's the same as with people. Animal babies, too, are often defenseless and dependent on the care provided by adults. Mammals rank as the most attentive parents because they feed their young with milk, but fish, reptiles, amphibians, birds, and insects also have some diligent parents. And by the same token, you can find some mammals who don't look after their young very well.

WHO WILL TAKE CARE OF US?

When it comes to animals, fathers usually don't take part in rearing their young. They simply produce offspring with their chosen partner and then go after their business. Mothers are left to provide all the care, education, and rearing. However, there are couples that divide the care equally among themselves. Penguins, for example, do it quite cleverly. Good exceptions also include seahorses–the males carry their young in their pouch until hatching. ◂

MEMORIES OF CHILDHOOD

An animal's childhood can last entire years (for example, with chimpanzees) or mere months and weeks. It depends on many factors: how developed the offspring is at birth; what its environment is; whether a parent or an entire group takes care of it; or what parents want to pass on to it before it grows up. For example, the young of marsupials are born undeveloped and must spend a significant amount of time in their mother's pouch, where they drink milk and grow stronger. On the other hand, the young of zebras and giraffes can walk within an hour of being born–otherwise, they'd be unable to get by in the rough savanna! ▸

THE PARENT OF THE YEAR AWARD

HOW MANY OF YOU ARE THERE?

The young's upbringing often depends on whether the animals live alone or in a group. The lonely ones meet their partner only for mating; otherwise, they arrange everything on their own. For example, alligator mothers rely only on themselves. Others live in groups and help each other with rearing the young: grandmas, sisters, older brothers, even aunts twice removed lend a helping hand. That's how elephants, wolves, or meerkats do it–they divide tasks among each other, which protects them from danger. ▼

AND THIS IS MY AUNT WHO TAUGHT ME HOW TO CATCH MYSELF A SNACK...

YIKES!

BAD PARENTING?

Not every animal mom is diligent and loving. Some abandon their young as soon as they are born. There are even those who eat their own children! As horrible as this may seem, there's a reasonable explanation for everything. Many young are born developed, with innate instincts that tell them what to do. But sometimes, a baby animal is born at a time when the mother can't get enough food, or the baby is weak and sick and wouldn't survive for long. In that case, it may happen that the parent steps in. ▲

Providing protection

Getting food

THE APPROACH TO UPBRINGING

Most parents try to pass on to their offspring everything they'll need once they grow up: getting food, defending themselves from enemies, or taking care of their own young. Some parents, such as chimpanzees or oystercatchers, show their children how to crack a nut or open a shell. Cubs of many predators fight and tease each other to practice fighting and hunting. The main thing is that they keep all these things in mind! ◄▼

Maintaining relationships

EMPEROR PENGUINS

A FAMILY OF GENTLEMEN

When you see these handsome fellows, you should take off your hat: not because they're all dapper in their little tailcoats, but because they manage to take care of their young even in the most challenging circumstances. Cold, hunger, enemies: they deal with all of these when raising their tiny penguins and properly preparing them to live in the rough Antarctic wilderness.

IT ALL BEGINS WITH AN EGG

When the mom lays an egg, she rolls it over to the dad's legs and sets out for a very long journey towards the sea. She's starving and can spend up to two months hunting. The upbringing is taken over by the diligent father. When the right time comes, the little penguin hatches. As soon as it's born, it starts **screaming** and wakes up all the unhatched young around. Thanks to this, all little penguins in the entire colony are born almost at once! ◂

THE NANNY

The dad becomes a full-time parent. And he takes his role very seriously, indeed! When the baby is still in its egg, he keeps the egg nice and warm on his own feet, covering it with the excess skin of his belly so that it doesn't touch the ice-covered ground and doesn't get blown upon by the cold wind. Once the baby is born, he feeds it with a **curdy substance** that forms in his crop. He joins forces with other dads and forms a group with them to keep all the young warm. ▸

CHANGING OF THE GUARDS

Hurray! Mom has arrived! That's a sign for the dad–the guards has changed and now he can go out to look for food himself. Since he lost almost half his body weight during the mom's absence, he's looking forward to his trip indeed. Meanwhile, moms give the tiny penguins their first real meal, pieces of the fish they've caught. ▸

FAAAAAALIIING!

FIRST STEPS

As soon as the tots are too big to fit into the mom's brood pouch, they must take a step toward their new life–literally! In order to stretch their legs, they practice walking on the mom's toes at first. They're unstable, just like all toddlers. Fortunately, their **down** softens all falls. Before the kids gain some confidence, they mimic the mom's style. After that, they scamper around like pros. ◂

MEEE TOOO!

PULLING TOGETHER

When penguin puberty is over–which is about six months after the birth–the young stop getting their food from their mothers. Time to jump into the **sea**! They slide on their bellies into the water and go hunting alongside their parents. They've learned much from them already and thus are great swimmers and divers. Before long, they'll pass on their knowledge to their own children. ▾

PROBLEMS OF ADOLESCENCE

While they're growing up, penguins change in front of your very eyes. The cute fluffy ball turns into a **molting** punk rocker and then into a dandy in a waterproof coat. Molting, as this change is called, happens several times. ▴

AMERICAN ALLIGATORS

ARMORED GENTLENESS

Alligators look like natural tough guys. And they are! After all, they're kind of living fossils! They've inhabited this Earth for millions of years, survived dinosaurs and the ice age, and almost haven't changed the entire time. When it comes to children, however, you'd be hard-pressed to find more loving moms. So don't let their armored back and robust jaws fool you!

SINGLE MOM

Alligator **dads** don't exactly strain themselves when it comes to rearing their young. However, the mom makes it up to the little alligators thousandfold and takes proper care of them since the moment she lays the eggs! ▸

Preparing the nest

LIKE IN A FEATHER BED

Before the mom lays her eggs, she prepares a **nest** for them, sort of like a cradle. She lines it with various vegetation and mud to make it comfortable and hidden from the eyes of enemies. After laying the eggs, she doesn't sit on them like a chicken would but camouflages them and guards the nest from afar. Woe betide those who come anywhere near! ◂

Mom cab

COMING INTO THIS WORLD

When the time to be born comes, the young let their mom know. How? They start making noises that the mom can catch due to her great hearing, even through the shell. If the babies don't manage to break through the leathery shell with their **egg tooth**, she rushes to help them at once. ▲

WHY IS YOUR MOUTH SO BIG?

Small alligators are vulnerable, and so their mom must protect them. Even though they're instinctively able to swim since birth, the mom prefers to **put them into her mouth** and carry them to safety. It's good to err on the side of caution, after all! ▼

Proud mom

SAFETY ABOVE ALL

Those who dare to come close to the young are playing with fire because the alligator mom will attack them. Sometimes, she carries her babies on her back or calls them over and hides them inside her mouth. The most important thing is to **protect** them until they're big enough. ◂

MOM, I'M ALL GROWN UP

Moms look after tiny alligators for about two or three years until they're able to defend themselves and find their own food. Then, the young leave the safe environment of their home, go out to acquire experience, and go through all of the joys and sorrows of adult life! ▲

RED KANGAROOS

WALKING INCUBATORS

These Australian moms have a pouch on their belly for a reason. They're marsupials-a kind of animal that usually has a pouch to carry their young around in. Apart from this carrier, kangaroos also have strong legs and a tail because they're one of the few animals that move around mainly by jumping. Kangaroos are responsible parents-if the conditions are unfavorable or there's drought or a lack of food, they don't make babies and wait until they can be sure there's plenty of everything.

LET'S PLAY PEEKABOO

When the little kangaroo is about half a year old, it carefully peeks out of the pouch and starts looking around. After a while, it dares to climb out for a short time. This allows the mom to clean up the pouch a bit and take a rest. However, if she senses danger, she'll call the baby over immediately. You can often spot tiny kangaroos with their head hidden in the mom's pouch, either feeding or plucking up courage since they feel protected like this. ▼

MINI BABY

When a little kangaroo is born, it's about the size of a bean. Even though it's almost **undeveloped**–bare and blind–it climbs up the mom's fur, all the way into the pouch, where it stays for several months, like it would in an incubator. It slowly grows there and feeds on the mother's milk until it's large enough to peek out of the pouch. ▲

POCKET PALS

A kangaroo mom can have another baby even if she has one tot in her pouch already. She looks after each one of them differently, but diligently nonetheless. The tot gets milk, which is **more nutritious** than what its older sibling receives. Once they're both grown up, the older sibling watches out for the younger one. ►

HOP HITHER, HOP THITHER

First steps are always hard. And now imagine that small kangaroos must learn to **jump** right off the bat! It's no laughing matter. So how do they do it? Do they stand on their front legs? Do they get off with the right foot, or the left one? Soon they learn that they must use the strength of their hind legs and their tail as well. Then they jump around like nobody's business! ◄

BUSY HANDS ARE HAPPY HANDS

The mom likes to pass her time by playing with her kids. This makes their relationship all the closer. Boys often engage in fights (pretend, for the time being). Adult males often "**box**" each other to determine which one of them is the larger and stronger tough guy. But the girls don't avoid pretend fights either! ▼

COME CUDDLE UP!

Boys leave their mother after three or four years. Girls usually stay and become moms themselves. Before the kids become too big to stay in the pouch, the mom likes to sniff, lick, and cuddle them. After all, having such a close relationship has a great influence on a kangaroo. ▲

CHIMPANZEES

A LOT LIKE HUMAN PARENTS

This chimpanzee family isn't too different from many human ones. Could you believe that primates are similar to us in a lot of respects? There's a 97 percent similarity of DNA between chimpanzees and humans. And the likeness doesn't end there: they're immensely intelligent, have strong bonds with the other members of their group, and use an elaborate system of communication. And most importantly, chimpanzee moms look after their babies with great tenderness and spend all their time with them.

Group hierarchy

A NEW ADDITION TO THE FAMILY

When a baby is born to a chimpanzee mom, it's as **vulnerable** as a human one. For the first couple of months, the mom cares for it with great attention and constantly carries it around on her body. She provides it with protection and food and warms it up at night, as it tends to be cold in the treetops where they sleep in a nest. Once they cuddle up, it's all well and good. ▼

FAMILY BONDS

Chimpanzees live in large groups where everybody has their designated place. Brave dads are the most respected of all because they look after the group and guard it. Moms spend most of their time caring for babies. But older siblings and other relatives aren't left out, either–they often help the mom, play with the others, or maintain friendly relationships by combing the fur of other chimps and looking for a tasty snack by doing so. ▲

APE NURSERY

When the baby grows up a bit, mom carries it around on her **back**. The small chimpanzee ventures outside the mom's company only after about two years. It romps with friends, plays games with them, and learns everything important. However, it still sticks by the mom, never leaving her sight. ▸

BUSY HANDS ARE HAPPY HANDS

Small chimpanzees are very **playful**. They can climb as early as six months after they're born, and tree branches are their second home. They romp about with their friends but also explore everything around. Every leaf, pebble, or berry is of interest to them. The older members of the community look after them. After all, it's all fun and games until someone gets hurt. ◂

LEARN YOUNG

Small chimpanzees don't have to go to school–their mothers teach them everything necessary, like how to get food or which herbs to eat when one feels sick. Chimpanzees are **very smart.** They can create a rod to catch termites with and are able to crack tasty nuts with stones. Just show them how to go about it, and they'll pull it off themselves next time. ▾

WHAT DID YOU SAY?

Chimpanzees communicate using **sounds, facial expressions, and gestures**. When the group finds food, the members start making noises that the others know means a goodie is around! You can tell by their facial expression when they're happy, angry, or scared. There are gestures, as well–a friendly pat on the back, a consolation kiss, or an order to commence the scratching. Chimpanzees simply understand one another! ▴

MUTE SWANS

A DYNAMIC DUO

This family has it all figured out. Mom and dad look after their grey-brown brood equally. Did you know that swan couples stay together until death? Maybe that's why they treat their children with so much love. Both adults raise them lovingly, teach them everything necessary, and carefully guard them. Swan fathers can really get angry; it's not a good idea to mess with them, and it doesn't matter whether they're in the middle of a busy park or by a peaceful pond.

Swan's nest

A SWAN IS COMING OVER!

Before the mom lays her eggs, she must make a **bed** for them–a king-size bed, in fact. She uses her strong beak to carry various twigs, reeds, and other plants so that the eggs are as snug as a bug in a rug. And safe as well! When the mom lays the eggs–usually over the course of five to seven days–she sits on them until they hatch. The dad sometimes takes over but mostly prefers to watch out and make sure the family stays safe. ▸

WELCOME TO THE WORLD!

Both parents warm the eggs for about a month until they hatch. And here it comes! The shells are starting to crack, and tiny grey heads are peeking out of them. Once all the young are **hatched**, they immediately go cuddle up with the mom–that's how their wet feathers get dry and they can be warm and safe. A well-deserved rest follows. The babies must recharge their batteries–their first swimming lesson awaits them the next day! ◂

I'M TIRED

You might not believe it, but little swans can **walk, swim, and eat** soon after they're born. The day after their birth, the dad gives them the first swimming lesson, and he doesn't spare them at all! Each time, he covers a longer distance with them than previously so that the babies get used to the water. Once their energy is depleted, they climb on the mom's back and get a nice ride, safe from any danger. ▼

WHAT A RIDE!

I'M ON YOUR HEELS

The freshly hatched swans begin to follow around the very first thing they see. That's why their parents try to form as close a **relationship** with them as possible. They even "talk" to the eggs so that the young can recognize their voices. The parents want to make sure that the babies won't think their parent is just any duck that happens to pass by. As soon as the young hatch, they start carefully observing their parents to learn all important things from them. ◀

THE FIRST DAY OF FLYING

When swans are about six months old, their parents proceed to teach them to **fly**. First, though, the young need to diligently stretch their wings and strengthen their chest muscles so that they can become proper flyers. When the day comes, the parents show their kids how to fly several times, and then the little ones try it for themselves. ▶

OFF WITH YOU!

Once the young are about a year old, they're fully **self-sufficient**. Once they're almost white, the parents conclude that it's time to lay new eggs–the kids are all grown up, after all! The young are confused at first, but soon find a group of equally old swans to join. Who knows? Maybe they find their own life-long partner to build a nest with... ◀

INDIAN ELEPHANTS

LOVING GIANTS

Elephant calves have it all figured out. They're taken care of not only by their moms but also by siblings, aunts, and grandmas. That's because they live in a herd led by the eldest cow elephant. The group does almost everything together. The members journey to find food and water, play together, and maintain familial relationships. The bond between an elephant mom and her calf is one of the strongest you can find in the animal kingdom.

Calf's coming to the world

NO TIME TO WASTE TIME

The freshly born calf can stand on its own legs, walk, and drink its mother's milk only a couple of hours after the birth. Calves are quick learners. They soon join others to journey for food and water and start eating foods (for example, grass). Since they're incredibly smart and curious, they explore and discover the world around them with their **sensitive trunk**, which functions as a sort of a hand. Let's go on an adventure! Not too far from mom, though... ▼

IT'S A CALF, MOM!

Mom has to wait a good long while before the calf is born. She carries the baby in her belly for up to **two years**! When the calf is about to be born, other females gather around the mom and sometimes even assist her with the delivery. The baby isn't tiny–elephant calves can weigh up to 220 pounds. ▲

WHAT GOOD IS THIS?

Before the calves figure out what their trunk is good for, it takes a while. They look confused during the first week of their life, as if the trunk isn't under their control. They can even trip over it! However, they soon find out how useful it is: they can use it to lift things, spray water into their mouth, they shower with it on hot days, use it as a snorkel when they're underwater, greet and caress others, trumpet, have conversations... What a truly wonderful thing! ▸

Ways of using the trunk

LITTLE RASCALS

Elephant boys can be proper **rascals**, especially when they turn 12 and reach puberty. They're very similar to some human boys in this regard. They start to take an interest in girls and want to show off in front of them. This is why they often nudge other elephants to show them who the boss is. However, their mom or grandma is always nearby to pull their ear. Elephants can be incorrigible, though. In time, they usually leave the female herd and either wander around alone or join other young male elephants. ◂

BUSY HANDS ARE HAPPY HANDS

Elephant calves spend a lot of time **discovering** the world around them and playing various games. They're just like you–they like to play tag, splash water on one another, and even throw sticks. They nudge each other and "fight" imagined enemies. ▾

FOR EVER AND EVER

Elephant girls usually stay in their own herd until they die. Elephant cows simply pull together: they protect each other, learn how to take care of the young, and if necessary, are always there to help. Calves can **get stuck** in mud or fall into a pit. If that happens, they need their mom, grandma, or aunts to help them out. ▴

GIRAFFES

CAMOUFLAGED BABIES

Look at the herd of elegant giraffes. They run around African savannas, graze on tiny leaves, and enjoy beautiful views. The young are looked after mostly by their moms who provide them with everything they need: from milk and protection to life's lessons which allow them to survive in the savanna. Not even such a large animal can manage without its mom's help!

I'M FALLING!

A giraffe mom carries the baby in her belly for more than a year, maybe so that it can laze around a bit–not to exaggerate, but its delivery is rather rough. Giraffes give birth while standing, so the young starts its life by falling from the height of about 6.5 feet. As soon as it's out, the mom welcomes it by licking and cleaning it. ▼

FIRST STEPS

Life is tough on giraffe babies–that's how things are in the savanna. After the initial fall, new trials are waiting just around the corner. The young have to stand on their own legs, go to their mom, and have a drink of milk. Approximately an hour after its birth, the little giraffe **stands up on its own**. Its steps are wobbly, but don't worry–it won't take a day for the tiny giraffe to start running! ►

WHERE'S THE INSTRUCTION MANUAL?

TIME FOR A SNACK

A giraffe baby lives off its mom's milk for about half a year. After that, it starts looking around and noticing which goodies she eats. Giraffes usually feast on juicy **acacia leaves**. They spend almost the entire day grazing. It's hard work to fill your stomach when you're this tall! The young need to eat a lot in order to quickly grow up. The best morsels always grow all the way up! ▸

ENEMY AT THE GATES!

Any **lion** or **hyena** would love to have giraffe babies for dinner! It's a good thing that the moms have such a long neck. They can spot danger from afar. That's why they chase the young into tall grass to hide. The kids then watch from there to see how they themselves will fight off enemies once they're old enough. Moms know how to kick predators with their long legs, and rest assured, it hurts a bunch. ▾

IN THE NURSERY

When the giraffe babies are a little bit older, the moms enroll them into a **nursery school** of sorts. They gather the little ones together and go off alone to graze nearby. The kids play with each other, run around, and pull various jokes. The boys can "arm wrestle" with their long necks. These are the first lessons of their future independent life in the savanna. For now, though, the moms are still discreetly watching from the distance. ▾

SEE YOU, THEN

When they're about 2 years old, the giraffe young are sufficient enough to no longer need their moms' help. Why should they? Now they're the **tallest animals** around! Their mom has taught them everything they'll need in life. The boys become independent and go their own way while the girls hang around their mom's herd a little while longer. ▸

POISON DART FROGS

THE EXCEPTION THAT PROVES THE RULE

These multicolored frogs differ from other ones in more ways than just their beautiful coloration. Most frogs lay eggs, leave them immediately, and no longer think about them. Not poison dart frogs, though! They look after their eggs diligently and lovingly. What a rarity among amphibians!

LOOK AT OUR BABIES!

Happy frog couple

MOVING

As soon as **tadpoles** hatch from the eggs, the frog parents are up to their ears in work. As you know, siblings often squabble. And if that isn't enough, the frog ones are capable of eating each other! That's why the parents put them on their back and carry them to a new home, one after another. It's quite the climb, like if a human parent walked a flight of stairs with their baby, all the way up to the roof of a skyscraper. ▼

WELCOME TO THE WORLD

The male poison dart frogs "flirt" with their sweethearts, using their beautiful singing voice. The sound carries throughout the tropical rain forest and cannot be missed. The female that likes the song sets out in its direction–and a new couple is formed! The pair celebrates their love with a dance, after which the female lays eggs in wet leaves. The dad isn't idle either. He brings water to the eggs so that they stay wet, or he simply pees on them. And he watches over them closely... ▲

DINNER TIME!

The parents visit the babies in their tiny **rooms** each day. The mom brings them food because the tadpoles would be hard-pressed to find food for themselves this high up. This means that the parents have to constantly travel up and down, again and again. But what wouldn't a loving mom do for her offspring? ▸

I'M GROWING AND GETTING STRONGER

A frog's development is strange indeed: a small egg turns into a legless tadpole, but as it grows, it gradually develops all limbs until it finally starts resembling a frog. What a wonderful transformation! Who would have thought that the baby would really look like its parents in the end? Tadpoles develop over about two months, but it takes approximately a year for them to become as big as their parents. ◂

DO YOU THINK IT WILL TAKE AFTER ME?

Although poison dart frogs are tiny, it's not a good idea to mess with them. They let us and other animals know this with their bright coloration, which means one thing: don't eat me, I'm **poisonous**! But small tadpoles are neither poisonous nor colorful. They don't need to be afraid, however: as they grow, they become not only colorful but also as toxic as their parents. ▾

ADULTS

Within a year, the little eggs turn into beautiful frogs. The males carefully guard their territory. Woe betide the male frog that breaches it, because this causes a great **frog fight**! And of course, this fight doesn't escape the attention of family-coveting ladies. Let the courtship begin! ▴

WEDDELL SEALS

HARDY FAMILY

Life in frozen Antarctica is not all sweetness and light. Only truly tough animals manage to survive there. But this adorable family has it all figured out. Its members aren't afraid of the cold and ice. On the contrary, they use them to their advantage. However, the young need to learn how to do so as early as possible. That's why they grow up fast, get stronger, and learn everything necessary from their mom. They live in Antarctica virtually throughout the year, and so ice and snow become a part of their family as well.

LIKE IN A FREEZER

The mom carries her young in her belly for almost a year. The newborn must be really shocked when it's born and falls right into the snow and ice. It must be like being shoved inside a freezer! Because the young don't yet have subcutaneous fat that would protect them from the cold, they must quickly start drinking their mother's milk. They get fatter gradually, but at least they have shaggy fur since the very beginning. ▼

GETTING FATTER AND STRONGER

Seal milk is **very nutritious**; it's up to 60 percent fat! Just for comparison, cow milk is only about 4 percent fat. No wonder, then, that the babies soon become properly chubby. They have a lot of catching up to do, after all. When they are born, their flippers are too big and the young need to grow into them. The little seals look hilarious while flopping on the ice, but after a couple of weeks of hearty nutrition, they can weigh up to twice as much as when they were born! The mom, meanwhile, undergoes a slimming treatment. Well, anything for the kids! ▲

A FLIPPER HERE, A FLIPPER THERE

After the first week, the mom starts teaching the small seal how to swim. After all, it will spend much of its life **underwater**. The young often have no idea what they should be doing in the water. Should they stick a flipper in it? Their head? The mom frequently decides to go for a shock treatment–she simply shoves the baby right into the water. As soon as the baby realizes that it can swim under the surface if it holds its breath, everything is just fine. ▸

LIFE UNDER THE WATER

After approximately five weeks, the young seal stops drinking its mother's milk. It's high time for the baby to learn how to catch itself a snack. Seals are natural-born **swimmers** and **divers**. They can stay under the water for at least 45 minutes on one breath, and they can dive really deep. However, they can't forget to hollow out a breathing hole. They come back to it every time they need to take a breath. They cut it into the ice with their teeth, which is why the young are born toothed already. ◂

HELLO?

Did you know that seal families like to **talk** to one another? The mom and her pup always recognize each other. When the baby withdraws from its mom surreptitiously, she knows how to call it back. Their conversations are so loud they can be heard even when the family is swimming under the ice! ▸

HAVEN'T WE MET ALREADY?

HELLO, BEAUTY!

As soon as the kid is **self-sufficient**, the mom goes out to find a new partner to have another baby with. She's already passed the most important lessons on to her child; the little one can swim and cut its own breathing hole in the ice. There's only one thing left for it to do–find a partner to start its own family with. ◂

MEERKATS

A LARGE FAMILY

Just picture it–a meerkat family that's not just a mom, dad, and their babies. It includes all the grandmas, grandpas, aunts, uncles, and other distant relatives. Meerkats live in large groups where every member has their role. The group is led by the mom who gives birth to the young. However, she's not the only one taking care of them. Everyone lends a helping hand and nobody minds. After all, they know there's strength in numbers.

PLAYING HIDE-AND-SEEK

Meerkats retreat to **underground burrows** where they're protected from enemies and the rough desert weather. The whole group lives there. It's spacious enough, with many chambers that serve different purposes–bedrooms, bathrooms, even a room where meerkat babies are born. Those are blind, bare, and defenseless, which is why it's best for them to stay hidden until they grow up a bit. ▲

SUPERVISORS

When the young are about three weeks old, they venture outside the dark underground for the first time and peek out to see the sun. They don't go too far from the burrow, though, and there's always an adult who **watches over them**. If there's any danger lurking around, the adult takes the young inside his or her mouth and carries them back to safety. ▼

LIFE OUTSIDE

The young get slowly used to a life outside the burrow. They find out that when they start whining, the others pay closer attention to them and bring them food. While the young drink the mother's milk, they gradually begin accepting the food they'll be **hunting** for later in life. ▼

PLAYING AND LEARNING

Just like other young, meerkats love to **play**. They're very curious small animals. They like to fight as practice for the future, when they'll have to defend their territory. The skills will come in handy! The young also often try out what can and cannot be eaten; they chew on twigs, as well as pebbles. And as always, there's an adult supervisor watching over them. ▼

DAY BY DAY

A year after the babies were born, they're adults and become full-fledged members of the community. They follow a **daily routine**: get up, go outside, warm their belly, divide tasks among themselves, and go find a tasty snack. Someone stands guard so that they can warn the group against enemies. Others watch over the babies. Together, they manage to do everything, even chasing off a snake! ▼

ESSENTIAL KOWLEDGE

Once meerkats are big, they start going outside with their group, hunting for food, watching over others, and acting as a nanny for the newly arrived young. That's why it's so important for them to **learn** everything: standing on one's hind legs, for example, is no laughing matter and requires good balance. One's fur doesn't become free of parasites by itself, either. However, learning is exhausting and must be punctuated by short naps. ▲

SEAHORSES

A DIFFERENT KIND OF PARENT

Seahorses are peculiar creatures. Their head looks like a horse's head, their tail like a monkey's tail. However, they're actually fish! Seahorses differ from other fish not only in appearance but in behavior as well. They're slow swimmers and have an erect body, but mainly are one of the few animal species where males and females switch their usual parental roles: it's the father, not the mother, who carries the young in its belly. That's why seahorses are often called the shining example of parenthood. But is it deserved?

WHEN A BOY LIKES A GIRL

Before two seahorses in love decide to have a baby, they have a little mating **dance** to make sure their bond is strong enough. After the dance is over, the female lays eggs into her partner's belly pouch. The male fertilizes them and carries the eggs in his pouch until they're mature enough. Because there's a lot of them (the female can lay hundreds of eggs), his belly is pretty full. ►

NO TWO POUCHES ARE ALIKE

The seahorse takes good care of his eggs by bringing **oxygen** to them and gradually **salt water** as well. Why? To make them prepared for the outside world once they're born. The mom checks up on the male daily, just to make sure. When the babies are born, they leave the dad's pouch for good. It's not like with kangaroos. Once they're out, they stay out. ◄

LOOKING AFTER THE YOUNG

Do you think that the dad takes care of the newborn little seahorses as diligently as when he was carrying them around in his pouch? Sadly, no. When the little horses are born, they're fully **developed** and **self-sufficient**. Nobody will look after them ever again, which is why a new rule takes hold: "It's every man for himself!" ◂

IT'S UP TO YOU

Seahorses must watch out for predators and strong ocean currents too. The babies can be carried away by a current in a jiffy. In order to make it up to them at least a bit, nature gave them **armor** (they have bone plates on their skin), a **proboscis** (there's a small mouth at the end of their snout which they use to suck in food, like one would with a vacuum cleaner), and a **prehensile tail** with which they anchor themselves to coral or their partner. ▸

AGAIN AND AGAIN

Seahorse dads are really devoted to their lifelong task. Consider this: as soon as they let the babies out into the world, they start looking for a female to have new children with. It's necessary, though– although seahorses can give birth to hundreds of offspring, only about a fifth of them manage to survive the tough underwater world. ▾

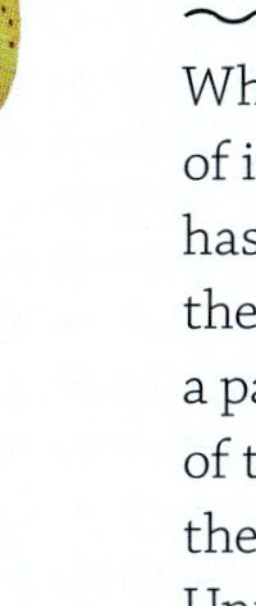

I'M ALL GROWN UP TOO!

When a male seahorse grows up and reaches the size of its parents, it can consider itself an adult since it has successfully overcome the dangers lurking under the surface of the sea. It's time to move on in life, find a partner, get pregnant, and release a new generation of tiny seahorses into the world. It's needed because the number of seahorses is **constantly decreasing**. Unfortunately, people are destroying their natural environment or hunting them too much. ◂

BLACK-BACKED JACKALS

A FAMILY THAT WORKS TOGETHER

These canine predators could serve as an example to other animals. The way they look after their family is simply incredible. The upbringing of the young is equally divided between the mom and dad. Even older siblings pitch in! One can survive the rough African savanna only by pulling together. The more jackal family members take part in the upbringing, the higher the chance that the next generation will greatly increase in numbers.

A couple in love

AN UNUSUAL COUPLE

Jackal couples in love faithfully stand side by side for **their entire life**. This is something one doesn't encounter very often in the wilderness. The partners are well coordinated and both of them take diligent care of their children. If they didn't, they wouldn't be able to raise more generations of little jackals. ◂

COZY HOME

The mom gives birth in the safety of her house: an **underground burrow**. She can have up to nine little jackal pups! To make sure they're all safe, they spend several weeks in the burrow. Since the pups are blind and toothless, the mom nurses, protects, and warms them up. Because she rarely leaves her home, the dad must lend a helping hand and get her something good to eat. ▸

TIME TO PLAY

When they grow up a bit, the pups go **outside the burrow** to explore. At first, they shyly stick their muzzle out, but soon they are fearlessly discovering the outside world. Pups love to play and can do so for hours: they tease each other, jump around, fight, and play tag. They develop their muscles in this way, but they also acquire the necessary experience they'll rely on once they reach adulthood. ▼

SUPER DAD

It doesn't take long for the pups to want something more nutritious to eat than the mother's milk. That's when the dad's time to shine comes: not only does he get food for the entire family, but he also tidies up, licks the pups clean, spends his time playing with them, and protects them. What a **super dad**, right? ◀

YOUNG ADULTS

Jackals often get help from their **older siblings**. When they grow up, they stay for about six months with their parents even though they could start their own family already. Why do they do this? By staying at home for longer than is strictly necessary, they gain protection and can practice hunting or defense against enemies more. They also learn to look after the young. When the young adults are about 18 months old, they're experienced and confident enough to move away from their parents. ▼

A HARMONIC COHABITATION

Jackals simply have it all figured out. When the whole family **pulls together**, everybody benefits. The parents don't have to worry about the little ones, the young adults learn to take care of pups, and the youngest ones learn and come to know everything they need. ◀

WILD RABBITS

ABSENTEE PARENT

Just look at this group of adorable, shaggy babies who laze about in their comfortable, warm nest. The nest was prepared by their mom so that the little rabbits would stay warm and safe. But wait, where is the mom going? Hello, Mrs. Rabbit, don't you want to spend time with your little ones?

I'M NO FAMILY PET!

ANY RESEMBLANCE IS PURELY COINCIDENTAL

Do you think that wild rabbits resemble your cute pets? It's no wonder if you do: they're the **ancestors** of all domestic rabbit breeds. But unlike our pets, they're much more **self-sufficient**. They're nocturnal, very social animals that live in colonies in complex underground burrows. ◀

ADVENTURES IN BABY GETTING

The female rabbit has young several times a year, from spring to winter. Yearly, she can give birth up to 30 adorable babies! However, she's the only one to provide them with an upbringing, as much as it can be called that. The male doesn't help at all. Before the mom gives birth, she prepares a bed for the babies and lines it with dry grass, moss, and fur she plucks from her own belly. The newborns will be quite snug! ▶

A RABBIT'S HOME IS ITS CASTLE

The complex system of **underground burrows** is occupied by several rabbit families at once. It's quite a maze. The burrows have several entrances, tunnels, and emergency exits. The older females inhabit the main "castle," while the lower status females build short dens at the edge to house their young. They're often disguised with grass so that the entrance stays hidden from enemies. ▼

Rabbit burrow

SAFETY ABOVE ALL

Rabbits are a delicacy to foxes, badgers, or weasels. That's why the mom leaves the tiny rabbits in the burrow once they're born and runs away. She returns to see and feed them only twice a day: at dawn and dusk. The entire meeting lasts just about five minutes, and then the mom dashes off once again. This is the only way to make sure that she doesn't leave her **scent** in the burrow, which might attract enemies to the little rabbits. ▲

A LONELY ADOLESCENCE

Since the young are born bare and blind, they are **easy prey** for all cunning predators. So let's have some understanding for the mom's tough teaching methods. However, since her milk is very nutritious, the tiny rabbits soon grow up. After three weeks, they're big and self-sufficient enough to do without their mom. ►

I CAN DO IT BY MYSELF

The grown-up rabbits are **well-equipped** to deal with the outside world: they have long, erect ears that can detect all imminent danger. They can hop to get away from enemies, and they find their own food. They're also instinctively able to hide from predators. What else would one need? When they're four months old, they can already start a large rabbit family of their own. ◄

HONEYBEES

ONE LARGE FAMILY

Insects usually aren't fans of rearing their young. Bees are one of the few exceptions. You'd be hard-pressed to find a larger family than theirs. Beehives house thousands of bees that live in well-organized colonies. Such a family works like a well-oiled machine: everyone has their task and tries to fulfill it to the best of their abilities. That's why a bee family grows very quickly! To find out the secret behind this great family dynamic, we must look inside. Let's go for a visit, then!

WHO IS WHO IN THE BEEHIVE

Each bee colony has a queen or a mother. Only the queen can lay eggs—sometimes up to 1,500 a day! **Worker bees** hatch from most of them. These do all the work. Some of them, though, can evolve into new queens. There are unfertilized eggs, too, and drones hatch from them. However, they live only a short time because their only mission is to have babies with the queen. ◂

WHAT DOES A BEE HOME LOOK LIKE?

Inside a beehive, there are honeycombs made from impermeable hexagonal cells. These chambers serve different purposes: some of them function as honey storerooms and are used mainly in winter when there's a lack of blossoms and nectar. We're interested primarily in chambers where **larvae develop**. These are the places where worker bees take diligent care of eggs and larvae to produce new bees! ▸

FROM AN EGG TO A BEE

After three days, a larva hatches from the laid egg. Its older sisters–the worker bees–feed it the most nutritious food that can be found in the beehive: **royal jelly** that makes the larvae grow, fatten up, and get stronger. After six days of being intensively fattened up, they're a thousand times bigger than before! Larvae from queen cells–the largest cells in the honeycomb where future queens hatch–are fed most of all. Then, the fattened larvae enter the pupa stage in their cell. After about 12 days, when the young bees are large enough, they bite their way out. ▲

QUEEN BEE

The queen's mission is to **lay eggs**. That's her sole job. She's surrounded by helpers–worker bees–who feed and clean her, make her comfortable, and generally ensure that she can focus on her main task. The queen bee works full time and lays eggs all day. Nobody can take over for her, so it's no wonder that she's treated like she's royal. ◄

A FUTURE OCCUPATION

As soon as the bees hatch, they become a **part of the colony** and are assigned a job. Worker bees are the largest group in any beehive since they have many functions: first, they clean up the cells of the honeycomb, then they feed the larvae, build new cells, air out the beehive, collect pollen, guard the beehive... Phew, being a worker bee isn't easy. ▼

MOVING AWAY

When bees reproduce, it's called **swarming**. The bee colony divides into two parts: one group, led by a queen, flies away to find a new hollow and build new honeycombs. The other group stays in the beehive where the new queen was born. I bet it has never occurred to you there are so many kingdoms in the world! ▲

Published in 2022 by Windmill Books,
an Imprint of Rosen Publishing
29 East 21st Street, New York, NY 10010

Author: Pavla Hanáčková
Illustrator: Linh Dao
www.albatrosmedia.eu

Cataloging-in-Publication Data

Names: Dao, Linh. | Hanáčková, Pavla.
Title: How animals care for their young / by Linh Dao and Pavla Hanáčková.
Description: New York : Windmill Books, 2022. | Series: Amazing nature
Identifiers: ISBN 9781499487541 (pbk.) | ISBN 9781499487565 (library bound) | ISBN 9781499487558 (6 pack) | ISBN 9781499487572 (ebook)
Subjects: LCSH: Parental behavior in animals--Juvenile literature. | Animal behavior--Juvenile literature. | Familial behavior in animals--Juvenile literature.
Classification: LCC QL762.H363 2022 | DDC 591.56'3--dc23

Printed in the United States of America

CPSIA Compliance Information: Batch BSWM22: For Further Information contact Rosen Publishing, New York, New York at 1-800-237-9932